Coming of Peacemaker

I would like to dedicate this book to Amos Christjohn and Maria Hinton of their endless work of compassion and love for their people. In teaching the language and culture, in giving us pride and appreciation for the sacrifice of opportunity in our people survival and moving forward in Peace.

I am going to tell you of the coming of the Peacemaker.

The Peacemaker as a boy was born in a Huron village near the Cave of Quinte on the banks of Lake Ontario. The events that took place during his birth was so sacred, that the name he was given is only used amongst the Council, to those who understand its great meaning, to the rest of Mother Earth he is known as the Peacemaker.

This was a time of great evil. The Iroquois hated their own blood. The endless battles and bloodshed was steeped in the foul stench of pure Anarchy. Many families ran into hiding. A Mother and Daughter also separated from the village, for the battles were ruthless and jeopardized their lives. They went into hiding and prayed for a better way of salvation for their people.

A young virgin woman was given a Message in a dream that she was going to conceive a child by the Spirit. Through this pure vessel the message of Righteousness, Peace, and Justice would be brought to the people, to unify them in oneness. The baby boy's name would be Deganawida. She was given instructions of him coming of age into manhood when it was

time for him to take the Message to the people so that no interference stood in his way.

The mother of the daughter was stunned when she was told the news of her conceiving. She pondered, how could this happen? I never let my daughter out of my sight. She interrogated her daughter with questions, but the daughter would not tell her of the dream or the messenger. The mother of the daughter came to the conclusion, this must be evil sorcery. In resolving the matter, I must take her further away from the village and kill the baby to remove the shame and save my daughter. Then we shall return to the village.

The birth of this baby was so precious, the grandmother was amazed at how different the demeanor and grandeur of the child was. The baby had a sweet, calming peace in his eyes. She could feel a powerful connection to the child.

She kept telling herself, if I do not remove this shame, it could destroy my daughter's life. I must save my daughter. She placed an herb into her tea to make her sleep heavy. While she was sleeping she took the baby.

Walking out into that cold morning, she held the baby close to her, afraid to look into his eyes and lose her nerve.

She kept repeating, I must save my daughter. She cut a hole in the ice-covered river and placed the baby into its current, whispering apologies to the Creator. With her fingers trembling in Fear, her tears froze to her cheeks she walked back into the lodge. A brilliant burst of light struck her with fear to see the baby back in the arms of its mother, safe and untouched.

She thought to herself, what power this child has! She thought and prayed, what do I do? How do I save my daughter? How do I destroy a child that the waters embrace? She thought, the fires of our Council holds great power. If he is of evil, the fires will consume him, and it will remove this evil once and for all.

The next day, the mother sent the daughter to go check their traps while she stayed to watch the baby. When the daughter was out of sight, the grandmother stole the baby. She went back into the woods to build a fire. Once again she held the baby close to her so she would not lose her nerve. She held the baby up to the sky and began to pray: Father we are good women under your order. We try hard to do good.

Please remove any wrongdoing we have done, I do not understand what is happening, please help my daughter. Remove any evil from us for we desire to walk before thee in righteousness and to return pure back into your circle.

As her body was shaking, she tossed the baby into the Fire. Just then a big bang struck the Earth and the Fire embraced the child. A whirlwind of Flowers made out of Flames devoured the child and the child disappeared. The grandmother fell to the earth and said, "The Fire became one with the child." In Fear she ran back into the lodge. There again, she found the baby in the mother's arms. Now she was really distraught. How do I save my daughter, she kept thinking. She thought, I have to return it back to the earth. I will dig a deep hole and cut the baby in half with a hatchet and bury it. A calm, peaceful Feeling fell over her and she went into a deep sleep. In her deep sleep, a spirit spoke to her in her dream and explained to her the great blessing that was bestowed upon her bloodline, and that this baby was sent to Mother Earth to bring the message of peace and to fulfill the promise the Creator gave our people. He was an answer to their prayers. Do not be afraid, for he has come to honor you and the power of your daughter. Help him to bring this message to our people.

The Peacemaker grew up good and he grew up strong.[11] Each day was a blessing for his grandmother and mother, witnessing his progression into manhood. Elements of Mother Earth were a constant reminder of his special mission to bring his people together as one. With each step, he prepared his heart with knowledge and understanding. At the age of seven he was ready to take on the responsibility of bringing forth the message to the people. In complete solitude, he poured out prayer for his people. The older he became in years, the more he understood the Creation. In responding to it he was able to do many great things. The grandmother and mother were impressed at the rise of his development, for he was a man now and they knew it was time for him to take the message to the people.

The mother said to her daughter, "I sense my grandson is preparing for his voyage. Let us go find him and see if we can assist him in any way." So they found him by the shore carving a canoe out of white stone. They silently kneeled down before him, waiting for his instructions. At the completion of the carving of the canoe, he rose up and said, "All things are ready. I must start my mission in taking the message to the people. I know I must travel Far to seek out the Council Smoke of Nations."

"This canoe that I carved out of White Stone will safely lead me to the sunrise. It will withstand the hardship of this trip to accomplish my destination." He went into great detail about the preservation of our people under this Great Message of Peace to stop the hatred of our people against each other, for this message is the reason why he was sent by the Creator. His grandmother and mother, with tears in their eyes, thanked him. "My life is dedicated to this mission. I will not come back here again."

His grandmother and mother acknowledged his great words as the waters carried his canoe down the river. They stood on the bank praying for a safe journey and that he would be given the strength to complete his great mission. They returned to their lodge in happiness, preparing to return to their village. As the Peacemaker crossed the waters, he read the codes in the water. The waters will speak to you, if you understand the codes. The Peacemaker learned the codes and had the ability to speak to the waters. It was the waters that directed him to where there was much evil in the air, a desire for killing and bloodshed. He saw men running on the shore. They saw the light of the white stone canoe and ran towards it for safety.

"Where are you going?" the Peacemaker asked.

"We saw light flicker from your canoe and ran here for safety. We are hunters and are running away from our village for there is much bloodshed among our people." The men then called out, "Who are you?"

The Peacemaker replied, "I have been sent by the Creator to bring Peace, Power and Righteousness to your nation. Go back and tell them I am here."

From the light that shone from him, he calmed the fear in their hearts and gave them Peace, for they knew that what he was saying was true. With excitement in their hearts they ran back to the village to tell the others.

As he advanced in an easterly direction the waters led him to a house of a woman who remained by the warrior's path, for this woman was very cunning. She would present herself in the traditional greeting of Friendship and gain their trust, allow them to rest, and when their defenses were down, she would poison them and kill them in the Food of Friendship. As the Peacemaker approached the house, he sensed that she would attempt to make him another victim. As she welcomed him, her eyes lied in greeting him. As he entered the house, the evil matter of the innocent lives swirled and whispered around her table. It confirmed to him what she was: a killer. As she set the food on the table with a smile, the Peacemaker said to her, "Why do the innocent lives that were taken cry from your table?" The smile immediately left her face, because she knew her treachery had been discovered.

She replied, "They take our innocence, so I take theirs."

The Peacemaker replied, "You will bring a new era. Instead of killing the chiefs, the instructions I was sent with say to organize our people to live for each other in oneness and avoid judgement to progress in peace. The instructions have three requirements: Peace, Righteousness and Power, and each section has two meanings. Peace in nuturing the body with Positivity, Strengthen the mind to love oneself. For Peace comes with oneness of body and soul. Righteousness is a proven system of true principles embraced by men and by nations. In a hope to overcome evil, for in religion, the intent of one's heart knows good from the bad and light from the darkness

For the Creator desires us to become like him. As a father desires the son to be better and become one with him.

For a promise that our chiefs in our Council Fire will withstand the winds of time.

That our prayers of our people will not be forgotten."

The woman said, "Your words are honest and true, and I will accept your message of Peace, Righteousness and Power. From this day on I will bestow this unto my soul and I will change my heart. I will apply it in my every day life.

I will vow to never return to my evil ways of destroying the chiefs."

The peacemaker replied, "Since you have changed your heart and accepted the Law of Peace, I will declare that it shall be the women who have the right of the title of chieftainship. They shall name the chiefs."

Tekarihoken is shown, The Great Law of Peace

    As the elements kept pulling the Peacemaker towards the Flint (Mohawk Nation), he approached the lodge of "the man who eats humans." Soon the man came home, hauling the remains of a human body, which was his supper. He dropped it into a big kettle held over a big fire. The Peacemaker wanted to calm the man's heart before talking to him. So he climbed on top of his lodge to get a better view. He lay flat on his chest peeking into the smoke hole. Just then, Tekarihoken bent over the kettle and saw the reflection of the Peacemaker's face. In seeing such peace in the reflection he pulled back in shock, "How could I have so much peace in my eyes when I take human life and use their body parts to obtain their power?" The Peacemaker knew that it worked. His seeing his face brought him peace. In his conscience, Tekarihoken said, "I must heal my heart and stop taking human life!" In understanding his heart, he knew it was time to teach him Truth. The Peacemaker climbed down and approached Tekarihoken, entered his lodge, and sat across the fire from him. "I am the Peacemaker. I am the one who caused the change in your heart to obtain the conscience to choose Peace. I am the messenger of the Creator, and the message is that all men should live together in peace, and live in unity based on a Law of Righteousness, Peace and Power. I will show you the sacred approach in hunting for your meal, for there are holy animals that the Creator placed on Mother Earth for you to eat. These bring you health and a strong mind for when minds are sane and bodies cared for and will bring you peace.

The Peacemaker left and soon returned with a deer. "I shall now cook this deer, and we will celebrate your meal in a feast to rejoice in your new heart and a new mind."

The Peacemaker spoke, "Because you have changed your heart and mind and realize how easy it is to do good, it is now time to put this great knowledge into action and apply it to your everyday life, to progress yourself and your nation forward. With your new mind you will build a Foundation of Peace and remove the Fear that is governing the people. Where it was once a weak nation, now you will make it strong.

Tekarihoken replied, "Because I have seen the facts that this Peace exists, in changing me, I know this is a proven system that works. The Peace has given me Power to go forward in righteousness. I am a New Man."

The Peacemaker told Tekarihoken that because he was the first man who accepted the "Great Law of Peace," he would make him the first "Sachem" in the Mohawk Nation. "Where once you hated your own blood, now you will live for others in Peace, Power, and Righteousness.

"The winds are calling to me to continue to the village of the Mohawk Nation, to which the hunters have returned to express my message of the Great Peace. I will offer my truth of Peace and Unity to that Nation. When they have change their heart, I will send for you to take your place in a Confederacy."

THE PEACEMAKER OFFERS THE LAW OF PEACE TO THE FLINT NATION

As the hunters arrived at the village of the Mohawk Nation, they informed them of the Messenager who was coming to meet with their Nation. "He is bringing the message of Peace, Power and Righteousness." As the sun rose they saw smoke coming from the open meadow at the entrance of the village. As was the custom in approaching a village of another Nation, a visitor had to build a fire letting the smoke act as a signal to the people that he wished to meet with them and that he comes in Peace.

Warriors were picked and instructed to approach and talk to him. To their amazement, their visitor was not bearing any weapons, but was sitting by his camp fire smoking his pipe and meditating. The Warriors then escorted the Peacemaker to the village to hear his message of Peace. After hearing the Peacemaker's plan for Peace and Unity, the Chief Warrior of the Mohawk Nation replied, "I agree that in order for our nation to go forward with "The Great Law of Peace" that a change of heart and a change of mind must take place to live together in Peace and Harmony, but where is the proof that this proven system will work? For us to lay our life down for "The Great Law of Peace" you must lay your life down for this truth. If you overcome death and come back to life this will give us a sign that this comes from the Creator. For if you are His messenger there is no death in you and you will live." Then, the Warriors Council selected a tree that stood by the falls. They instructed the Peacemaker to climb to the top of the tree. The warriors cut the tree, and the Peacemaker fell into the falls. If he should survive the test, they would accept the terms of his Message of Peace.

The Peacemaker agreed to the terms of the Chief Warrior of the Mohawk Nation, so the Peacemaker climbed the great pine and started praying, "Creator, Father, I've come upon our people who are set in their ways and way of thinking. I would never tempt your great power with my life, but they want a sign. Father guide this tree that my life will live and I will be able to deliver the message, which thou has sent me to deliver." As the Great Pine was cut down, it fell into the rapids of the falls. It missed all the boulders and was captured by the waves of the waters. For the waters knew him and guided the tree safely to an opening where the river calmed. He was able to get to the shore safely. The Waters spoke to him, "The people are hard in their hearts and are cold to change. For your safe passage you must stay in this meadow opening and pray for their change of heart." So the Peacemaker stayed in the opening of the meadow and prayed for his people. He also prayed in recognizing the Creations and the Great Circle of Life and the Truth that had been given to him to deliver to his people.

Meanwhile, back by the Mohawk people, they waited and watched to see if the Peacemaker came up, but there was no sign of him. With no patience, they returned to the village in despair.

The next morning, the people saw a thin trail of smoke rising in the direction of the entrance to the village. They all rushed to see if it was the Peacemaker. Women with tears in their eyes of hope ran with the children out front. Warriors helped the elderly men hurry to the spot of the smoke trail. As the morning sun burst out it rays through the trees, a group of birds encircled him and there he sat…The Peacemaker. In the arms of the warriors the elders were walked in front of his presence. The Chief Warrior of the Mohawk Nation looked at him and said, "I no longer doubt your message. You are the Peacemaker who has been sent by the Creator to bring us a plan of direction for a better way of life." Then, he turned to his people and said, "Let us become one, with the Good News of Direction of Peace, Power, and Righteousness." Without hesitation, the People of the Mohawk Nation accepted the Message of the Creator and became the First Nation to become one with "The Great Law of Peace."

The Peacemaker said, "This is why I was sent to Mother Earth, for it is your Right to become one with this message. For your bloodline holds a sacred treaty with the Creator. You are his people and He is your Father. Now let us start, for there is much to be done yet." He explained that on his journey toward the people of the Mohawk Nation, he was sent to an evil women and an evil man. "But because of the message that I brought to them, they changed their heart and accepted "Great Law of Peace." They will now use their Power to further the cause of Peace and Unity among your people." The evil woman dedicated her life for Truth and completely changed for good. She has gained the right of Chieftainship, where the clan mothers will have the right to select the Chiefs of the Nations. Tekarihoken is the first man to embrace, "The Great Law of Peace" into his heart and have healed his mind and soul. He has earned the right to be the first (Sachem Chief) of the Mohawk Nation. The Mohawk Nation became the first Nation to accept the terms of the Great Law of Peace.

HIAWATHA attempts to unify Ononadaga

The Peacemaker was uniting the Mohawk Nation in teaching them "The Great Law of Peace" in bringing their minds together as one. The people knew it was desperate times to make a choice to unite and live or be separated and die. Hiawatha went through a struggle in uniting Onondaga Nation.

In the Onondaga Nation hardship of battles had caused the peoples' hearts to become very heavy to where they were not united. Many times Hiawatha poured out his heart in prayer to the Creator of how to bring the people together in one mind and one heart. He knew if they continued in the fierceness of rage their bloodline would be wiped out, for the people lusted for battle. There was no peace among the Onondaga Nation. The nights were so dangerous they became prisoners in their own homes. Warfare, Sorcery, and Treachery ran rampant in a murderous fog that hung over their nation. Hiawatha knew of an evil-minded man who lived south of the Onondaga town. Snakes came out of his hair as a product of evil to strike Fear in his enemy, for his family and loved ones were wiped out and all he had left was rage. "Because they took the flesh of my loved ones and left me with only bottomless, loneliness, darkness. I will eat their human flesh and take their soul," Atotarhoh thought. He practiced bad medicine, "They want something to be afraid of…I will give them something to fear." His power was based on rage. Using these powers, he would destroy people. Everyone in the village feared him. Anything this man would say, the people would do, knowing that he had lost everything he ever loved and they pitied his despair. His conscience was void, refusing to ever care again. The snakes lived off his rage and bitterness in hating life. His sorrow of bottomless depression caused a sickness in his body that produced seven crooks of disformity. This man who lived off hateful rage and lonely depression was called Atotarhoh.

The power of Atotarhoh's influence over the Warrior Society was remarkable, for he was the last of his bloodline. "A wrong had to be made right," said the elders, "We can't move forward without honoring the sacrifice of Atotarhoh's relatives. We need him if we are to move forward. How do we heal Atotarhoh's heart?"

The Onondaga Council was frustrated from trying to find the direction they should take in uniting the Onondaga Nation. They called a meeting a Hiawatha's lodge. They discussed how Hiawatha had tried before to clear the mind of Atotarhoh. "The loss of your family and the evil that was done to you, Atotarhoh, it does not call for the evil you are sending out," Hiawatha said,
"The wrong that has been done to me in wiping out my
bloodline is a never healing wound. You know not of the grief that has inflicted my heart. The hearts of our men are weak. How can we advance in weakness?" Hiawatha had no answers for Atotarhoh and left troubled and confused. Knowing the meeting was a failure. The Council decided they had to keep trying to negotiate with Atotarhoh, to obtain unity and move forward.

The men who were picked were not in unity of mind for obtaining oneness in meeting Atotarhoh. They argued and complained about why they were being sent. Atotarhoh could smell their negative attitudes and could hear their conversation. When they were in the middle of the river, Atotarhoh saw them and yelled to the people, " Stand up and look behind you, for there is a strange storm that is after you." The men yelled and argued with each other, and moved in a disorderly fashion. They rocked the boat and overturned it. They fell into the river, and many drowned in fear; few escaped. The survivors returned to the village in defeat. Again, Atotarhoh had proven to them their lack of oneness.

The second time they tried to meet with Atotarhoh, they thought, we will outsmart him. Half will stay on land and half will go by the river, but stay close to the shore, for fear of his powers over the water. Again, Atotarhoh knew of their arrogance and that they would come to complain. He saw the smirk in their eye on being on the land. "We have him beat out of the water. He has no control on land to stop us. He will obey and come with us to the village. Enough of this wasted energy coming all the way out here." They complained amongst each other. Atotarhoh sensed in his mind the conversation and connected with the feeling of the men and felt the rebellious behavior in their mind. He knew they were not one. Because of their pride he knew what would distract them, so he tested them. He yelled to the Warriors to look at the eagle that had been flying up in the sky. Atotarhoh released dark matter to choke the eagle that was flying, killing it. He had the feathers fall from the body. They floated down towards the warriors. The lust of Pride filled the Warriors' eyes as they tackled each other, "I can use that for my ceremonial dress," one hollered, "I saw it first," another one yelled as he wrestled his fellow brother for the feather. The selfishness in only thinking of oneself, caused fists in to start flying among the Warriors, they were so heated, beat up, and infuriated with each other. They completely forgot what Hiawatha instructed them to say to Atotarhoh. The Warriors stormed off, walking with, busted eyes and embarrassed of their behavior. They knew that their, true heart was revealed before Atotarhoh and the second attempt to meet with him failed. As they walked away defeated, Atotarhoh sat their laughing, "Nice try" chuckling at how foolish they were.

The next day Hiawatha called the people, "We must solve this matter with Atotarhoh. We must control the situation. He is making fools out of us. Don't let him trick you." At the time the people were counseling with Hiawatha, another group was having a meeting. They were listening to a certain great dreamer. This person had dreamt that there would be a man coming who would be travelling from the north and pass to the east. "Hiawatha, you must go and meet this man! You must unite with him and go to Mohawk Nation together, for I saw it in the dream. Only there you will obtain the information we need to make our nation one. You must go!" The Dreamer told the people that Hiawatha must not remain with the Onondagas, but must go to the Mohawk people. When the time came for the journey to be made to go see Atotarhoh, there was a division within the people, "Everything we have attempted in meeting Atotarhoh has failed. Maybe the information we receive from this man will give us the direction we should take." the council said. More and more they understood the great meaning of the Dreamer's dream and that they needed to listen and obey the direction it gave, but Hiawatha was steep in pride and stubborn in thinking, "No, I feel this way is better. I feel I must stay here and resolve the matter with Atotarhoh …first!" he demanded. "I cannot leave my daughters. I cannot leave my property." A man of the Council rose up to speak to Hiawatha, "You are honored as a leader among us… You made a oath of marking your skin into our Warrior Society. You marked your skin to always put us first. You marked your skin to lay your life down for us. We come… before your daughters! We come…before your property! We among the Council, among the Warrior Society… it is We, that is your property. Now we beg you, go and represent us and follow the Dreamer dream of direction for it comes from the Creator. Go and find this man and accomplish the great task in uniting with him in Mohawk Nation." This man, hands open, pleaded with Hiawatha, but Hiawatha was upset he was called out and would not swallow his pride. His ears were closed and his eyes shut. "I will not GO!" he said and left the meeting. This left the Council upset. In despair they continued to discuss what could be done. "To be apart of the Warrior Society you must be held accountable of your actions. The people must come first!" The Dreamer's Council and followers agreed to employ Ohsinoh, a famous sorcerer.

Hiawatha had seven daughters in whom he took great pride and whom he loved very much. In his vanity of their beauty, he refused to allow any of them to marry, believing that no Warrior was good enough for his daughters. The Council knew that with the removal of the daughters, Hiawatha would suffer much sorrow. "You cannot worship your children and put them before your duties of your oath to the people!" one elder said. "If Hiawatha removes the worship of his daughters, entrusts them to marry, and allows his bloodline to carry among our people, their husbands can care for them and protect them. He then can carry out this great task in putting his people first. No harm will come to them, but their safety is based on Hiawatha swallowing his pride." Still, the Council thought this was the only way to make him free to leave, and that in thinking of the welfare of the people, he would forget his own sorrow.

Hiawatha tried, but could not call the people together. They refused to listen to him, "We will not listen to you, until you listen to the Dreamer and go to Mohawk Nation to speak to this man." They said. The Dreamer's Council had become successful.

That night, Ohsinoh climbed a tree overlooking Hiawatha's lodge and positioned himself on a large limb, Filling his mouth with clay, he imitated the sound of a screech owl. Ohsinoh called to the youngest daughter and sang, "Unless you marry Ohsinoh, you will surely die." After this, he climbed down and went home as he was instructed. Within three days, the youngest daughter strangely died. Hiawatha grieved, but still would not swallow his pride. While he was in sorrow, no one came to comfort him. The five other daughters passed away, each in the same manner and still Hiawatha would not swallow his pride and listen to the council and travel up to Mohawk Nation and meet this man. Instead Hiawatha's relatives became angry and in their anger became suspicious as to why so many daughters of one family met their death without cause. They began to suspect that evil in the form of witchcraft was being used against the family of Hiawatha.

These relatives, instead of sitting Hiawatha down and counseling him to be obedient to the Dreamer's dream, they sought revenge for him and desire to beat the guilty one to death. They rallied at Hiawatha's lodge during the daylight hours. When evening came, they were ready. They knew nothing of Ohsinoh's sorcery. They only suspected that a wrong was being done in hate and jealously towards Hiawatha household.

That night the moon was silent and there was no light when Ohsinoh appeared. He crept in out of the trees so familar to the lonely darkness of the night, switching his eye sight to the owl he showed no fear. He drove the staff he had in his hand right into the ground. He was snorting, like an animal in drawing black matter into himself. Then, he climbed the tree. In his pocket he had clay which he put into his mouth and started to chew. When he had chewed it for a few mintues, he spat it out, then imitated the sound of the screech owl.

    He sang his famous song, "Unless you marry Ohsinoh, you will surely die." As the morning hours came, Ohsinoh began his climb down the tree. As he touched the ground, one of the men shot an arrow and hit him. Ohsinoh fell to the ground and saw that they were coming to club him to death. He shouted to them, "In the power of screech owl, you are unable to club me, for there is no power in your arms." Just then they froze from the power of the screech owl. When they tried to club him, they couldn't lift their clubs, for they had become very weak. Ohsinoh also told them, "Today, I will heal myself from this wound."

    Within three days, the last daughter died. Now, because of Hiawatha pride and worship of his daughters, all seven daughters of Hiawatha had died because of the evil practices of Ohsinoh. Hiawatha grieved. He was in pain with sorrow of his mind and heart. No one came near to console him.

His grief was so deep that he lost hope for happiness and resolved to leave the Onondaga Nation and become a woodland wanderer. Hiawatha mind was covered by a cloud of unanswered questions, he departed from the Onondaga Nation. He journeyed toward the south, and that night, he camped on a powerful mountain where he offered up prayers for his people. This was the first day of his journey. On the second day, he camped at the bottom of the hill. On the third day, he carried forward his journey, and that evening he camped in a hickory forest. He called this grove "Onenokarensne". The next morning, he found a place where the joined rushes grew. He made three strings out of the joined rush plant. He called this plant "Oseweneste". As he attached them, he put some words together saying, "If I found or met anyone burdened with grief as I am, I would console them. I would lift the words of condolence with these strands of beads, and these beads would become words with which I would direct and speak to them to heal and to comfort." As evening came, he stayed there, and named the place after the plant.

As the sun light burst the new day, he continued his journey. After praying for his people he felt that he should alter his direction. He turned east. That night, he felt the water call to him, some small lakes where he saw a flock of ducks in the water. There were so many swimming together they appeared like a raft.

Hiawatha said to himself, "If I am to be a leader among men in showing them how to heal themselves , I need to focus my mind on being a respecter of life, understanding the light that is within me for turning on my powers." Then, he spoke out loud and said, "All you ducks who have been created by the Creator, I know you are one with the land, water, and sky. The element of water listens to you. Lift up the water and allow me to cross, for I am a respecter of life."

The ducks immediately flew up together so swiftly that they lifted the water with them. Hiawatha walked across the dry bottom of the lake. As he was crossing, he noticed layers upon layers of empty shells fresh water clams. Some of these shells were white, and some were purple. So he bent down and filled his deerskin pouch with them. He pushed on, crossing the lake until he arrived on the other side. Then, the ducks returned and replaced the water. It was on this fifth day that he began to obtain healing of his heart, and Hiawatha finally became very hungry. So he killed some game and ate.

The next morning, he ate the meat that he saved from the night before. Then, he resumed his journey. This was now the sixth day, and he hunted for some more small game to eat. Then, he rested for the night.

CONDOLENCE OF HIAWATHA

The seventh morning, he pressed on in his journey and turned south again. Late that evening, he came to a clearing and found a bark field hut. This was where he spent his night. He made two poles, stood them up and added three shell strings. Looking at them, he said, "Men do a lot of boasting, but never do what they say. A change of heart is a change of mind in how you change your life.

"If I should see anyone in deep grief, I would take these shell strings from the pole and console them, in uplifting their souls and showing them a better way of healing their mind and improving their life. These strings would become words that would lift away the darkness with which they are covered." Again, he said, "This I would surely do."

Meanwhile, a little girl was playing a short distance away, and she noticed the smoke rising from the hut. So she crept up and listened to what was being said. She turned quickly and ran home to tell her father of this strange man. "The stranger must be Hiawatha," said the father, "I heard he had left the Onondaga Nation." The father told his daughter to return to this man and to invite him to their lodge. The girl did as she was told, and she returned with Hiawatha. The father asked him to attend an Oneida Council. It was many days later when Hiawatha left the meeting and continued his journey into the woods. Again, he was hurt, and sorrow fell upon him. For this man had invited him to council with the Oneidas, and yet, no one ever said one word to him. Not one discussed the matter of his losing his seven daughters nor consoling his grief. No truth of the matter was discussed and no answers were given to Hiawatha. This was now the tenth day. He came to another Oneida settlement, so he kindled a fire as was the custom of visitors and travelers in those days. When he was settled in, he erected two crotched poles. They stood upright in the ground and were connected by one horizontal pole which rested in their crotches. On this horizontal pole, he hung his three strings of wampum, and repeated his words of condolence. The Chief Warrior of the village saw the smoke at the edge of the forest and sent a messenger to see who the stranger might be. When the messenger arrived, he saw the stranger sitting by the fire in front of the two poles. With a very humble behavior he waited patiently. He heard Hiawatha as he was reciting his words of condolence, determined to bring light to anyone trouble with grief. When the messenger saw that Hiawatha was finished, he was troubled and wanted to help in Hiawatha campaign in uplifting others in their grief. He hurried back to tell the Head Warrior what he had seen and heard. The leader of the village immediately realized that this must be Hiawatha who he heard had left the Onondaga Nation. "It is he who shall meet the great man (the Peacemaker) foretold by the Dreamer," the leader said, "We have heard that these two men shall meet one day and establish peace among all the Nations."
The Leaders sent the messengers back to invite the visitor (Hiawatha) into the village.

The Oneidas greeted Hiawatha and asked him to sit on the Council and listen to the discussion. So Hiawatha sat down and listened. Seven days went by, and not one word was spoken to him. The people talked without motive to cure the problem, no answers arriving at any decision, to know what direction to take in overcoming and moving forward in resolving the problem. No report was officially made to Hiawatha, so he did not hear what they talked about.

On the eighteenth night, a runner arrived from the South, from the Nation residing on the seashore. He told the Leader that they had heard of the Great Hiawatha from the Onondagas, and of how a great man had come to reside near the Mohawk river at the lower falls. The runner said that they also heard that this great man from the north (the Peacemaker) shall meet another great man from the south. Hiawatha must now change the direction of his journey and go east to the Mohawk Nation. The Oneida Leader himself went with the party of four to escort Hiawatha, for he understood the destiny of the power of these two man meeting to bring order in saving us from Chaos. The journey lasted five days, and on the fifth day, the party stopped and camped near the village where the Peacemaker was staying.

The Mohawks greeted the visitors and escorted the party into the village. When Hiawatha entered, he told Tekarihoken that he was there to see a very great man who came from the north. Tekarihoken answered, " Here are two warriors who will escort you to the house of the Peacemaker." The two warriors went out and took Hiawatha to the Peacemaker's lodge. This was on the twenty-third day.

HIAWATHA MEETS THE PEACEMAKER

The seven daughters strangely dying, was a great loss for Hiawatha. The heart ache in not having the answers was a constant piercing pain. Hiawatha explained that he felt he could only wander, because of the doubt it brought to himself and his outlook on his people for he felt he had no belonging. Looking for his purpose, he searched the forest in deep prayer, ever since he had left his people at Onondaga. The Peacemaker told Hiawatha to stay there with him and that he would tell the people of that village what had happened. Finally, Hiawatha had found someone who listened to his sorrow and suffering and who wanted to give him answers. The Peacemaker began to tell the people what had happened, and everyone listened. The five warriors were now dismissed. Hiawatha gave thanks to each one and told them they were the connectors who made the connection to him and the Peacemaker in order to receive the answers about his dispair. Now he could obtain peace of mind, and soul. In all gratitude, desiring only to help others, the Oneidas returned home. The Oneida Warriors said, "It has now happened, what was foretold in a dream. The two are now together. Let them now arrange the Great Peace." Then the Warriors departed. At this point, the Peacemaker brought the trouble before the Council, He promised to let Hiawatha know of their decision. The Chiefs talked about the tragic events and finally they agreed to do as the Peacemaker suggested. The Peacemaker would approach Hiawatha and help him overcome his sorrow. The Peacemaker went back to the lodge of Hiawatha.

As he was about to enter, he heard the words of Hiawatha addressing the strings and saying the words of condolence. When he finished, the Peacemaker went into the lodge and said to Hiawatha, "My younger brother, it has now become very clear to me that your sorrow must be removed. Your grief and anger has been great, but I will give you the understanding that shall remove your sorrow so your mind may rest." The Peacemaker asked if he had plenty of shell strings. Hiawatha answered, "Yes, I have plenty of shells in my deerskin pouch." He opened his pouch and the brilliant purple of the wampum fell out. The Peacemaker said, "I shall string eight more parts to my address to you." Hiawatha allowed the additional stringing so, in all, there were fifteen strings of wampum. He bound them in four bunches. "These will be used to console the one who has lost by death a near relative. Overcoming the evil act will help in obtaining a reality of righteousness to apply, to be able to go forward and heal oneself," the Peacemaker said to Hiawatha, "The fifteen strings are now ready on the horizontal pole, and I will now address you."

   As the Peacemaker addressed Hiawatha, he would take one string of wampum off the pole and hold it in his hand while he talked. After each part of his address, he would hand one over to Hiawatha. The words that he spoke to Hiawatha were of the fifteen condolences 1.) Wipe away the tears of grief 2.) Clear one's eyes of distress 3.) Resume the breath of peace 4.) Relieve the twisting within the body 5.) Wipe away red marks from one's space 6.) Bring life over the darkness of grief 7.) While the sky clears-let's watch for peace 8.) Restore the sun-remember peace 9.) The grave cover restores the mind 10.) Elevate the mind through the land 11.) The Council Fire rekindles the peace 12.) The Faithkeepers' tent 13.) Calm the insanity of the mind 14.) Replace the torch of the community 15.) Installation of the good mind.

When the fifteenth ceremonial addresses had been made by the Peacemaker, the mind of Hiawatha was finally made clear. He was now satisfied, and once again, saw things rightly. The Peacemaker then said, "My younger brother, these fifteen strings of shell are now completed. In the future, they shall be used in this way. They shall be held in the hand to remind the speaker of each part of his address, and as each part is finished, a string shall be given to the bereaved Sachem on the other side of the fire. Then shall the Sachem hand them back one by one as he gives a reply. It then can be said, 'I have now become even with you.'"

As the Peacemaker addressed Hiawatha, "My younger brother, now that your mind is clear and you are competent to judge, we shall make our laws, and when we have finished, we shall call the organization we formed THE GREAT PEACE. It shall have the power to end war and robbery between brother and bring peace and quietness. You shall wear deer antlers an emblems of your Sachem titles. As we are approaching Atotarhoh, we shall sing this song. When he hears it, his mind will be made straight releasing the destructive darkness from his eyes and make his thought pure. If we sing this Peace Song without making any mistakes from beginning to end, then we have succeeded." Hiawatha agreed. Then, the Peacemaker told Hiawatha that it was time to bring this plan before the Mohawk Council, to determine if it would be okay to proceed with the plan.

So the Peacemaker explained to the Council about establishing a oneness of all the nations. He told the Council that the Chiefs must have a love for the people and willingness to lay down their life for the people to be virtuous men and very patient, kind and understanding in wisdom. They should wear deer antlers upon their heads as emblems of their positions, because he explained that their strength came from the meat of the deer. Hiawatha then confirmed all that was said.

A speaker of the Mohawk Council told both Hiawatha and the Peacemaker that they would have to send the message to the Chief of the Oneidas and ask their Council to consider the plan also. So, when the Chief of the Oneidas was told, he answered they would get their answer tomorrow. Well, tomorrow, according to the time of the Creator, was one year later. After the Oneidas considered the issue, they agreed that they would join the confederation. Then, the Mohawks sent two more messengers to the Onondaga Nation and asked them to consider the proposal made by Hiawatha and the Peacemaker. It was during the summer when the messengers left the Mohawk Nation territory to approach the Onondagas about the proposals they had. When the Onondagas received the message about the proposals, they asked that they wait for one day for an answer. The two warriors went home and waited for one year before they got a reply. When they did receive their answer, the Onondagas agreed to the proposals and that they would be the Firekeepers of the Confederacy.

At about the same time the message was sent to the Onondagas, the Cayugas also received it. The Cayugas also waited for one year before they gave their answer, which was that they were in full agreement with the proposals. They had one more Nation to approach which was the Seneca Nation. So, they were two runners who were picked to go and deliver the message of the proposal. The Senecas took one year to consider the matter. They could not seem to be of one mind when they were considering it. Half of the Council would agree with the proposal, and the other half would not. When they finally came to a conclusion, they told the Mohawk Nation that they accepted the proposals of Hiawatha and the Peacemaker.

The Peacemaker said to Hiawatha, "Now we have contacted the Five Nations and have all their approvals. It took us five years to get all the Nations to agree. I will now report back to the Mohawk Nation."

THE HEALING OF THE KAIANEREKOWA (GREAT LAW)

The Peacemaker asked the Mohawk Chiefs to call a Council. Messengers were sent out among the Mohawk people and the meeting began with the Peacemaker stating, "I, with agreement from Hiawatha, wish to report what we have accomplished these last five years. We have received the consent of the Five Nations: the Mohawks, the Onondagas, the Oneidas, the Cayugas and the Senecas, to have oneness in mind to become strong nations. The next step is to seek out Atotarhoh. Atotarhoh's bloodline is of crucial importance in moving forward. What happened to him was wrong. We need to make it right in helping heal his heart. We must find him."

The Mohawk Council agreed with the Peacemaker and Hiwatha's report. They sent a member each of the deer and bear clan to find Atotarhoh and report their findings upon return to the Mohawk land.

After the two messengers left, the Peacemaker addressed the Council and said, "I am the Peacemaker and with me is my younger brother. We will now lay before you the Laws which will form the foundation of the Kaianerekowa. The symbol of the chiefs shall be the antlers of the deer. The titles shall be the responsibility of certain women and the names shall be held in their clans forever." The Laws were recited and Hiawatha agreed with them.

The Song for Conferring a Title was then recited by the Peacemaker. All the work and plans for the Kaianerekowa were reported to the Council and Hiawatha confirmed it all. The Council then adopted the plan.

The two representatives sent to find Atotarhoh returned and reported their findings to the Council. They reported Atotarhoh had seven crooked parts, his hair was infested with snakes and he was a cannibal. This was the result of the rage and despair which had infected the people's heart in having no direction. The Council heard the message and after much discussion the decision to go to Onondaga was made. They must help heal Atotarhoh's heart. They would leave at midsummer.

There was time to learn the Hymn of Peace and other songs from the Peacemaker, for singing was a declaration of the Heart being true. He taught the songs to many of the Mohawk people and the Mohawk people learned the songs in preparation for their trip to Onondaga to carry the Great Peace. As the time drew near to leave for Onondaga the Peacemaker chose one person to sing the song before Atotarhoh, in declaring that we come with one heart and one mind. This singer led the people through the forest as he sang the Songs of Peace. Many places were passed as they went through the Mohawk Country. Entering the Oneida country, women and children would meet them in respect of their diligence. The elderly women would bow and honor their determination to bring the nations as one. The Great Chief, Odatshedah of the Oneidas, met with the Mohawk Council and the Peacemaker.

The Oneidas joined the Mohawks and together they continued the march to Onondaga with the Singer of the Peace Hymn leading. Deer would line up in honoring them. The echo of their oneness rejoiced through the trees as the birds landed around them to witness the great event.

When they reached the Onondaga territory, the Oneida and Mohawk leaders stopped and built a fire as was the custom in proclaiming coming in peace. The chiefs of the Onondagas and their head men met with them and all joined to march to the fireside of Atotarhoh, the singer of the Peace hymn leading the Mohawks, Onondagas and Oneidas. At the home of Atotarhoh, a new singer was selected to sing the Song of Peace. As he walked towards the door of Atotarhoh singing the Peace Song, he was reminded that he could not make an error or hesitate in his singing or else his Power would be weakened and all would be lost with Atotarhoh, for he would know his heart was weak. Thinking about such a matter made the singer hesitate, so another singer was appointed who made the same error as the other singer.

To assure peace among the nations, the Peacemaker sang and walked before the door of Atotarhoh's house. A Burst of light came from the Peacemaker's mouth as he sang the Hymn of Peace. The tone in each word comforted Atotarhoh heart in releasing the demons from his ears. The intelligence of light went into his eyes and awakened him. When he had finished his song, he walked towards Atotarhoh. He rubbed Atotarhoh's body for him to know the strength and life he possessed. When finished, Atotarhoh's seven crooked parts became straight and hair was free of the snakes. Tears of joy shook Atotarhoh body, for he knew he was no longer a prisoner of the demons of doubt and fear. With Atotarhoh new heart and of new mind, the establishment of the Great Peace could take place.

The Peacemaker then spoke to those assembled. He said, "Each nation must select a certain number of their wisest and kindest men to be the Chiefs, Rotainer. These men will be the advisers of the people. They will sit in Council and make the decisions for their respected nations. The women holding the hereditary titles, Clan mother, will make the selections and confirmations. Once named, the Chiefs shall be crowned with deer antlers to symbolize their positions.

The Mohawk women titleholders brought forth nine men for Chiefs. Next, the Oneida women titleholders brought forward nine men for Chiefs. The Onondaga women brought forth fourteen men to become Chiefs. The Seneca women brought forth eight men to become Chiefs. Finally, the Cayuga women brought forth ten men to become Chiefs. After this ceremony took place, each Chief was then responsible for delivering a string of wampum a span in length to the Peacemaker as a sign of Truthfulness and Sincerity.

Now the Peacemaker spoke to the chiefs and those people assembled. He explained that these men would no longer have the same names but greater ones. They would each have antlers as a symbol of their position. In their position, they would receive much abuse so the thickness of their skin must be seven spans. Each of you must work for the people. To live for others in laying down your life for the People. There must be unity so that no one can hurt one Nation without hurting all. Always think in terms of the generations to come, for our bloodline must go forward. Your authority comes from the Great Peace which each Nation has pledged to uphold. In bringing our minds together as one.

The Great Peace Law which was devised by the Peacemaker and Hiawatha was then read to the Five Nations assembled and the Confederacy was established.

ISBN-13: 978-0-9988513-7-2
ISBN-10: 0-9988513-7X
© 2017, BURDEENA CROSSETA ENDHUNTER
ENDHUNTER ORIGINALS
JOHN E.POWLESS JR
CALAWAY JAMES CHRISTJOHN
BURDEENA CROSSETA ENDHUNTER
PUBLISHED BY PHIA STUDIOS © TEELIA PELLETIER
ALL RIGHTS RESERVED

www.ingramcontent.com/pod-product-compliance
Lightning Source LLC
Chambersburg PA
CBHW041538220426
43663CB00002B/73